J. Barrett

A description of Malvern and its environs

comprising an account of the efficacy of the Malvern waters

J. Barrett

A description of Malvern and its environs
comprising an account of the efficacy of the Malvern waters

ISBN/EAN: 9783742840646

Manufactured in Europe, USA, Canada, Australia, Japa

Cover: Foto ©knipser5 / pixelio.de

Manufactured and distributed by brebook publishing software (www.brebook.com)

J. Barrett

A description of Malvern and its environs

A DESCRIPTION
OF
MALVERN,
AND
ITS ENVIRONS.

COMPRISING
AN ACCOUNT OF THE EFFICACY OF THE
MALVERN WATERS,
AND
THE ACCOMMODATION OF STRANGERS IN THAT
DELIGHTFUL NEIGHBOURHOOD.

A SKETCH
OF
THE NATURAL HISTORY
OF THE
MALVERN HILLS,
AND
CONCISE ACCOUNT
OF THE
GENTLEMEN's SEATS, SCENERY, AND PICTURESQUE
VIEWS IN THEIR VICINITY:
WITH MANY OTHER INTERESTING PARTICULARS.

BY THE REV. J. BARRETT,
OF COLWALL.

Worcester:
PRINTED FOR THE AUTHOR BY T. HOLL.

1796.

A DESCRIPTION, &c.

CHAP. I.

THE SITUATION, EXTENT, AND HEIGHT, OF THE MALVERN HILLS DESCRIBED — SOME ACCOUNT OF THEIR COMPONENT MATTER — CONJECTURE RESPECTING THEIR STATE IN REMOTE ANTIQUITY — SKETCH OF THEIR SURFACE.

IT appears that the MALVERN HILLS have been long diftinguifhed by that title; but, according to the rules of geography, they will not properly bear the appellation.—The *ftrata* in thefe elevated tracts are arranged in a per-

perpendicular direction, which is the discriminative mark, or characteristic, of a mountain, always attended to by those who have treated scientifically of that branch of knowledge. However, since the name of *Malvern Hills* is rendered familiar by custom, I shall speak of them under that denomination.

* * * * * * * * *

These eminences are situated in the several counties of Worcester, Glocester and Hereford; environed on the east by an expansive plain, and on the west by an uneven, but fertile tract of country. They are about eight miles south-west from Worcester, twenty east from Hereford, and fourteen north-west from Gloucester. Their geographical situation is in about 52 degrees of north latitude, and one hundred and fifteen miles north-west, or 3 degrees longitude

longitude weft, from the meridian of London.

The Hills extend about nine miles in length; namely, from Leigh-Sinton, in the county of Worcefter, to Bromfberrow, in the county of Gloucefter; the former being the moft northern, and the latter the moft fouthern, extremity.

Their breadth is very unequal; fo much fo, that it varies from one mile to two miles, and upwards.

The higheft parts are thofe diftinguifhed by the names of the Herefordfhire and Worcefterfhire Beacon, probably fo called from their being ufed as fignal places, when the adjacent country was the theatre of military achievements. Thefe elevated protuberances are about four miles diftant, and fituated in the refpective counties, which diftinguifh their appellation. The Herefordshire Beacon was formerly computed to be the highest point of the hills; but by an accurate mensuration, the Worcestershire Beacon is found to be something higher; the former being about twelve hundred and sixty, and the latter about thirteen hundred feet, perpendicular height from the surface of the adjacent level.

The component matter of the Malvern Hills, principally consists of a mass of stone of various kinds; but which is in general so rugged and brittle, as renders it unfit for carving, or being applied to any valuable purposes. About two-thirds of the mass is granite, a silicious substance of a grey colour mixed with veins of red. In some places this stone can be raised in blocks of a considerable magnitude, but rarely without a mixture of some heterogeneous matter. It is of an exceeding durable nature,

nature, and poffeffes the chymical property of refifting acids. Both the grey and the red takes a good polifh, and the latter then fomewhat refembles cornelian.

The hills contain a confiderable quantity of quartz, fmall pieces of which may fometimes be found perfectly exempt from any other fubftance; but in general it is united with the granite into an aggregate body. This is a fpecies of flint of a whitifh colour; it ftrikes fire with fteel, and refifts acids.

Exclufive of the various kinds of ftone that compofe the *ftrata*, are contained a great variety of calcarious, mineral, and argillaceous fubftances, detached in maffes among the rocks, or depofited in veins in the incumbent beds of gravel.

The

The moſt remarkable of theſe productions is a large maſs of ore, lying in the ſummit of the hill, about one mile to the ſouthward of the village of Great Malvern.——This ſubſtance is rather ponderous, therefore no doubt was formerly entertained but that it might be productive of ſome kind of metal. Hence, about the year 1715, a ſmelting houſe was erected at a ſmall diſtance from the ſpot, by one Williams, of Briſtol, and furniſhed with proper utenſils for the purpoſe of refining the above mineral ſubſtance.—But this proceſs could not be effected; in conſequence of which, the building was taken down, and of courſe the buſineſs wholly relinquiſhed.

Now it has been aſſerted, that the miſcarriage proceeded from a deficiency of ſkill in the workmen who were employed in the operation; and that it it was still practicable to be brought to some degree of perfection. But this assertion has been refuted by recent experiments, which have proved this substance to be a kind of mica, not fusible by any process whatever.

Though this is the precise nature of the ore, taken at no considerable distance from the surface of the hill; yet the interior parts may contain ore, not only fusible, but even valuable. That this is the case, has been the opinion of several gentlemen conversant in mineral researches; and likewise of the ingenious Dr. Wall, of Oxford, who in a note to his appendix on the Malvern Waters, makes the following observation:—" Whatever metallic sub-
" stance this hill may be found here-
" after to conceal, many circumstances
" lead us to imagine, that if the re-
" searches formerly undertaken should
" ever

"ever be renewed, and purfued with liberality and unremitting perfeverance, the exertions of the proprietor will not be unrewarded. It requires no common degree of patriotifm, and the affiftance of great wealth to profecute fuch enquiries. Hence many fpots, which have been generally believed rich in mineral productions, have been neglected for years, from the parfimony or timidity of their poffeffors."

It may be proper to obferve, that the trials, made about the year 1715, were never carried to any great extent, being in fome meafure cramped by the narrow circumftances of the proprietor, who in the courfe of this bufinefs expended about fix hundred pounds; which is faid to have been nearly the whole of his property.

Among the above-mentioned ore is found that curious production afbeftos; an inconfumable matter, which is well known, and was much efteemed by the ancients.

In one part of the Hills I obferved a fmall quantity of fpar lying in the foil, or gravel, about two feet below the furface: It was hard and quite pellucid, and formed in hexagonal chryftaline figures.

That beautiful elevated ground called Old-Caftle Bank, which branches out of the hill, and extends in a tranfverfe direction about a mile to the weftward, is chiefly compofed of water ftone; a brittle fubftance, not fufficiently durable for the exterior purpofes of building. When it is applied to the repair of the public roads, or long

expofed

exposed to the weather, it dissolves to a greyish soil, that is said to be favourable to vegetation.

The western declivity of the Hill contains a bed of limestone, which is the course of a vein that commences near Pensax, in the county of Worcester, and terminates at Ledbury, in the county of Hereford. It produces excellent lime, at least in the vicinity of the Malvern Hills, where large quantities are made annually; particularly in the parishes of Colwall and Mathon. This stone, which is of a blue cast, is interspersed with veins of a whitish colour, which together take an excellent polish. It is sometimes used for chimney-pieces; and, when properly finished appears little inferior to the Derbyshire marble.

In

In the above limestone are an almost infinite variety of marine productions, particularly the remains of shell-fish; such as cockles and muscles, of various sizes; some of them partly, and others of them wholly, petrified, or changed to a perfect limestone. I have likewise seen the fragments of different kinds of fish, in a state of petrifaction, but retaining their natural figure. These *strata* also abound with the relics of several kinds of zoophites, a most singular marine production, which are always found in a petrified state, and are commonly known by the name of screw-stones. They are the remains of substances that possessed animal and vegetable life, and which are therefore considered by naturalists, as the grand concatenation of the animal and vegetable kingdoms. I have recently discovered in this limestone the fragment of a horn,

horn, which probably belonged to a cornigerous marine animal.—It is in a petrified state, but not totally divested of its original testaceous matter. Here is also found the *cornu-ammonis*; specimens of which I have seen of different sizes, but always divested of their native shell.—I have likewise found the *nautilus*, the head of an exceeding large *encrinus*, several species of gryphites, corals, *fungi marini*, &c. Many of these marine relics are in great preservation; the shell-fish retain their *striæ*, and the other kinds their respective *vertibræ*, with their figures so extremely perfect, as leave no room to doubt of their species, and incontestibly prove that they belonged to the aquatic element.

It undoubtedly exceeds the limits of human abilities to demonstrate the origin of the Malvern Hills, or to ascertain the period of their existence.
Never-

Neverthelefs, it is obvious that they are either primary productions of nature, or were produced at fome very remote æra, and might probably have been rocks involved by the ocean.—This latter idea, at the firft perception, may appear rather romantic, till it be recollected that the globe has fuffered various revolutions, and that its furface, in many parts, has undergone a fimilar alteration.—Thofe marine productions contained in the limeftone, as before recited, form the principal bafis of this conjecture. The method of their arrangement in the *ftrata* evidently fhews, that they were thus depofited by water: hence thofe parts muft have been pervaded by that element. That vaft aggregate mafs, or rock, which compofes the Hills, is perfectly exempt from any marine production; an indication, not only of their primary exiftence, but,

C that

that they had acquired their folidity previous to the limeftone. It was before obferved, that the remains of zoophites, by fome termed fenfitive plants, were extremely numerous; which fubftances, when in a living ftate, always inhabit the cavernous receffes of rocks in the fea, fuch 'places only being adapted to the nature of their exiftence—hence the difcovery of thefe relics pleads ftrongly in favour of the conjecture. The beds of limeftone which contain thofe marine bodies, when the water fubfided, (which might have been either at the grand deluge, or fome fubfequent period), were probably banks of foil, which, from being faturated with water, were fubject to petrefaction. Therefore, it is prefumable, that this law operated progreffively to the production of the limeftone, and the prefervation of thofe adventitious fubftances.

Various

Various other productions of the natural kingdom, abound in the environs of the Malvern Hills, from which inferences might alfo be deduced to illuftrate the above conjecture; but natural hiftory not being my peculiar ftudy, nor its fubject the defign of the prefent treatife, I fhall, therefore, refer that detail to thofe more converfant in fuch difquifitions.

The more elevated parts of the Malvern Hills, which are not enclofed nor cultivated, chiefly belong to proprietors of land in the adjoining parifhes. The furface, in fome places, is productive of gorfe and fern; in others it is a fweet turf, affording an excellent fheep-pafture:—Large numbers feed thereon, and the mutton, which is fmall, is much efteemed for its mild flavour.

CHAP II.

AN ACCOUNT OF THE CAMPS—DIMENSIONS OF A CAVE IN THE HILL—PARTICULARS OF THE DISCOVERY OF A CORONET, OR CROWN OF GOLD—DESCRIPTION OF BRANSEIL CASTLE.

On that part of the Malvern Hills called the Herefordſhire Beacon, are the remains of an old camp; but by whom it was formed, or at what period of time, cannot be aſcertained, as there is no hiſtory extant that mentions the circumſtance: but it may be conjectured that it was formed at a very diſtant period; if not before hiſtory was known in Britain, yet before any progreſs

Various other productions of the natural kingdom, abound in the environs of the Malvern Hills, from which inferences might also be deduced to illustrate the above conjecture; but natural history not being my peculiar study, nor its subject the design of the present treatise, I shall, therefore, refer that detail to those more conversant in such disquisitions.

The more elevated parts of the Malvern Hills, which are not enclosed nor cultivated, chiefly belong to proprietors of land in the adjoining parishes. The surface, in some places, is productive of gorse and fern; in others it is a sweet turf, affording an excellent sheep-pasture:—Large numbers feed thereon, and the mutton, which is small, is much esteemed for its mild flavour.

CHAP II.

AN ACCOUNT OF THE CAMPS—DIMENSIONS OF A CAVE IN THE HILL—PARTICULARS OF THE DISCOVERY OF A CORONET, OR CROWN OF GOLD—DESCRIPTION OF BRANSEIL CASTLE.

ON that part of the Malvern Hills called the Herefordshire Beacon, are the remains of an old camp; but by whom it was formed, or at what period of time, cannot be ascertained, as there is no history extant that mentions the circumstance: but it may be conjectured that it was formed at a very distant period; if not before history was known in Britain, yet before any progress

gress was made in that science; otherwise it is probable, that history would have afforded us some information concerning its origin. Some have imagined that it was a Roman or Saxon, and others a British camp. The latter opinion seems to carry the appearance of most probability; for it is natural to suppose, that when the Britons were driven by the Romans beyond the Severn, they posted themselves in some situation where they might be able to make a stand, and repel the further progress of their enemies. Now the Malvern Hills being advantageously situated for that purpose, they probably availed themselves of the eligible position. The existing remains of this camp consist of two intrenchments, or what is usually termed a double ditch, formed in a circular direction round the declivity of the eminence. The uppermost, which is very near to the

the summit, is about seven hundred feet in extent. The other is formed lower on the descent of the hill, and is much more extensive, being upwards of half a mile in circumference. These trenches are from six to twelve feet deep, and in some places more than thirty feet broad, and supposed capable of containing an army of twenty thousand men. The avenues or passes are still to be seen, and the greatest part is in fine preservation.

On a protuberance of the Hill, about a mile and half further to the southward, are the remains of another camp, consisting of only a single ditch. The form and appearance of this, seem to bespeak that it was not made by the same people as the abovementioned; and perhaps was formed at a more remote period.

On

On the declivity of the Herefordshire Beacon, at a small distance from its summit, is a cave cut in the rock rather of an oval form, but of rude workmanship and small dimensions. The entrance is about four feet wide, and six feet high. The concavity, or hollowed part, is ten feet in length, six feet broad, and seven feet high. It is unknown for what purpose, or by whom this cell was made; but it is not unlikely to have been the retreat of some recluse individual.

A notion has long prevailed among the inhabitants of the adjoining country, that much treasure has been lost or deposited on the Malvern Hills; but from whence such an opinion originated I am at a loss to conjecture. However, a quantity of silver coin was found about forty years back on the west side of the Hills, in the parish

parish of Mathon. It is said that it amounted to a considerable value; but I could never procure any further particulars of it. But the most valuable, as well as singular discovery, was the coronet, or crown of gold, and its appendages, mentioned by Camden, and other writers and historians. There is a manuscript account of the particulars of this discovery, kept in the library of Jesus College, Oxford, of which the following is a copy:—

"Within the distance of a musket
" shot of the trenches of the camp,
" in the parish of Colwall, in Hereford-
" shire, was found, in the year 1650,
" by Thomas Tailer, near Burstners-
" cross, as he was digging a ditch
" round his cottage, a coronet, or
" bracelet of gold, set with precious
" stones, of a size to be drawn over
" the arm and sleeve. It was sold to
"Mr.

"Mr. Hill, a goldsmith, in Glocester,
"for 37l. Hill sold it to a jeweller in
"Lombard-street, London, for 250l.
"and the jeweller sold the stones,
"which were deeply inlaid, for 1500l.
"as Mr. Clough, of Lombard-street,
"reported."

It has been supposed that the gold alone of this coronet, might have been worth about 1000l. which, added to the value of the diamonds abovementioned, amounted to the amazing sum of 2500l. This curious relic should certainly have been preserved as an invaluable piece of antiquity; but being only in the possession of mechanics, and of such great value, profit prevailed against curiosity; therefore it was soon demolished, even before the discovery was made public, or any of the learned got the inspection of it. The opinion of some is, that this was the diadem
of

of a British prince, who might have been slain in some contest not far distant.

It appears from the registers of Colwall, that there were several of the name of Thomas Tailer, lived there about the year 1650. On examining the deaths, I found the entry of two of that name, one who died in 1654, and another who died in 1661. In the margin of the register, opposite to the name of the latter, is perfixed an asterisk, which, in all probability, was inserted, both to distinguish that this was the person rendered memorable by the above discovery; and also as a reference to some particulars made relating to it.

On the declivity of the Malvern Hill, in the parish of Eastnor, are the ruins of Bransil Castle. A vestige of the wall is the only part remaining of this ancient structure, which was fortified with

with a double ditch faced with ftone. The appearance of this venerable ruin immured in wood, together with the obfcurity of its fituation, and ftillnefs of the furrounding water, fills the mind of the beholder with a contemplative melancholy. I have not been able to obtain information at what time it was erected, or who was its founder; but the general opinion is, that it was built by the Britains, foon after the Romans left this ifland. Some ancient records, I am informed, fhew, that this caftle came to the crown by forfeiture, from the Earl of Dorfet; and that Henry VI. granted it to the great Talbot, Earl of Shrewfbury. It afterwards became the property of the Reeds, of Lugwardine, in the county of Hereford; from a defcendant of which family it was purchafed about the year 1778, by Charles Lord Sommers, the prefent proprietor.

CHAP.

CHAP. III.

OF THE HOLY WELL, THE EFFICACY OF ITS WATERS, AND THE METHOD OF USING IT—SOME OTHER SPRINGS TAKEN NOTICE OF—DESCRIPTION OF THE LODGING HOUSE—EXTENT AND BEAUTY OF THE PROSPECTS FROM THE MALVERN HILLS—ACCOUNT OF THE RIDES IN THEIR VICINITY.

A Variety of springs rise from the Malvern Hills, some of which are uncommonly pure, and others are impregnated with different substances.—Experience has proved that many of these springs are serviceable in various diseases; but there is one called the Holy Well, that is allowed to be more eminently salubrious, which has attracted peculiar attention.—This

This rises on the east side of the Hill, in the county of Worcester; distant two miles from the village of Great Malvern; and is the source of that much esteemed clear element, called Malvern Water. From whence this spring derived its appellation is not certainly known; but tradition says, that it was in great repute with the antients, who ascribed the virtue of the water to a supernatural effect, communicated by some celestial benefactor; and therefore this well was dignified with the epithet, *Holy*. It is probable that the title thus originated; at least, however, the above assertion is not repugnant to the superstitious notions which prevailed in former ages.

The medicinal virtues of this water have been repeatedly experienced by the afflicted; not only among the inhabitants of the neighbouring country, but by invalids who have come there from different parts of the kingdom. It has proved fingularly beneficial in fcrophulous cafes. Objects thus afflicted, have arrived at Malvern in the moft deplorable condition, who foon found relief, and in no long time were perfectly cured, by the conftant ufe of this falutary water. It has feldom failed of being ferviceable in moft diforders of the eyes; and there are many inftances of its having effected a cure in thefe complaints, when the prefcriptions of fome very eminent of the faculty had proved ineffectual. This water has alfo proved very beneficial to people afflicted with cancerous complaints, and old ulcers, whom it has reftored to foundnefs, health, and vigour. It is likewife efficacious in moft cutaneous diforders; alfo in glandular obftructions, and nephritic complaints: but, though the water has been found more peculiarly

culiarly fuccefsful in the cure of the above difeafes, yet it has proved ferviceable in a great many others.

The numerous cures of dangerous complaints effected by this water, prove, beyond a doubt, that it poffeffes a powerful efficacy; but from what origin this quality proceeds has not, perhaps, been clearly afcertained, tho' various trials have been made for that purpofe. The moft general opinion formerly was, that it arofe from a mineral impregnation; but that idea has been long fince refuted by a variety of experiments, made or fanctioned by Dr. M. Wall, of Oxford, who, in his Treatife* thereof, concludes, " That from the whole of the experi- " ments contained in his appendix, it

* This TREATISE may ftill be had of MR. HOLL, *Bookfeller*, WORCESTER.

" appears that the Holy-Well water,
" at Malvern, does not contain any
" uncombined vitriolic acid, nor any
" volatile alcali, nor any metallic falt;
" that it is flightly impregnated with
" fixed air, fome common air, fome
" felenites, and fome unneuteralized
" calcarious earth. Hence it is obvi-
" ous, that the principal virtue of Mal-
" vern water, muft depend upon its
" extreme purity, affifted by the fixed
" air which it contains."

Doctor Johnftone, an eminent phyfi-
cian in Worcefter, informed me, " That
" he had made experiments on the
" Holy-Well water, but could not find
" that it contained any fixed air; that
" his experience had confirmed its great
" efficacy in fcrophulous cafes, cuta-
" neous eruptions, and alfo in nephritic
" complaints; and this efficacy he af-
" cribed to the great purity of the
" water

"water alone." He moreover obferved, "That the temperate warmth of the air, "and great purity of the water at Malvern and its vicinity, induced him "to confider that fituation peculiarly "adapted for patients afflicted with "nervous diforders, or inclined to confumptions; efpecially in the fummer "or autumnal months."

It may be proper to obferve, that in moft complaints for which the water is prefcribed, it muft be ufed both by drinking and lotion. In fcrophulous and fcorbutic complaints, bathing the whole body and drinking freely of the water are exceedingly neceffary; and in ulcerous diforders, the methods of admitting the water into the affected part as it falls from the fpout, and the application of wet linen, are found the moft beneficial.

Early

Early rising, and a proper degree of exercise, either by riding on horseback or walking on the Hill previous to using the water; and also at intervals afterwards should by no means be omitted; as such exercise in that pure air will promote a due circulation, and indeed prove a powerful auxiliary in the cure of those diseases, for which the Malvern waters are recommended.

The source of the Holy-Well is secured by a decent building, containing a bath and several apartments suited to the various purposes that using the water require.

Near the village of Great Malvern is a spring that affords a lightly impregnated Chalybeate water, of which kind this is perhaps the most free from earthy or calcarious matter of any that is produced in Great Britain. It has proved eminently

eminently ferviceable in confumptive complaints, nervous diforders, and emaciated conftitutions.

The late Dr. Wall, of Worcefter, fays, " It feems to challenge one of
" the firft places amongft the waters
" of this clafs. For though it be not
" fo highly impregnated with iron as
" fome others, yet it is fufficiently fo
" to anfwer all our expectations from
" it as a Chalybeate; and being much
" lefs loaded with earth than others,
" it feems probable that the ferruginous
" particles will for that reafon be more
" readily and intimately mixed with
" the blood and juices, whilft the
" water, by its extreme purity, per-
" vading the fineft veffels, wafhes away
" the accrimonious falts and obftruct-
" ing vifcidities.—This water at the
" fpring head inftantly ftrikes a fair
" purple with galls; and if carefully
" taken

" taken up and clofe corked, will
" retain the fame property feveral
" hours; but the colour grows gra-
" dually more and more pale, and at
" the laft approaches to the orange.
" To have this water, therefore, in full
" perfection, it muft be drank at the
" fource."

On the weft fide of the Hill, in the parifh of Colwall, is a fpring called Moorarls Well, that affords a water, which has proved ferviceable in fcrophulous cafes. Here a building containing a bath is erected near to the fpring, for the convenience of people who ufe the water.

There is another fpring on the weft fide of the Hill, called Walms Well. This water is much efteemed by the neighbouring inhabitants, who affert that it is beneficial in a great variety of diforders

diforders, and particularly in cutaneous complaints. It is faid that this water contains fulphur, from which, it perhaps derives that falubrity for which it is celebrated.

There are two other fprings rife from the weft fide of the Hills, the one in the parifh of Colwall, and the other in the parifh of Eaftnor, which have a petrefactive property. This is evident from the mofs and vegetables immerfed in their ftreams; which, for a confiderable diftance from the fprings, are incrufted with a lapidious matter. Thefe concretions are of various fizes, fome of them feveral inches in diameter, and are the effects of a calcarious matter contracted by the water, in its current through beds of limeftone.

At a fmall diftance from the Holy-Well, is a commodious Lodging-houfe, at prefent kept by Mr. Steers. It is a well built ftructure, fituated on the defcent of the Hill, commanding extenfive and beautiful profpects. This is chiefly the refort of genteel company, who generally board and dine together in a large room, and are fupplied with excellent accommodations. It is feldom vifited in the winter, the air here being very fharp in that feafon: but in the fummer this fpot is moft delightful, rendered particularly fo in the morning, by aurora's enlivening afpect and the rifing fun; whofe meridian rays are tempered by refrefhing breezes, peculiar to the Malvern Hills. It is a fituation defirable to the healthy; but highly fo to invalids, who here enjoy a falubrious air and water, the beauties of nature, and in fome degree, the tranquillity of retirement.

Near the above lodging-house are several delightful walks on the Malvern Hill, which, by a gradual ascent, lead to its summit, where, in addition to the local beauties, the eye enjoys most expanded prospects. From hence are seen ten counties, namely, Monmouth, Radnor, Hereford, Brecknock, Stafford, Salop, Glocester, Worcester, Oxford, and Warwick; some of them appearing uniform by distance, and others beautifully diversified by art and nature. Here the cities of Glocester, Worcester, and Hereford are visible; several market towns, and with the assistance of a glass near a hundred churches. It is extremely delightful to behold the surrounding country from hence, in the months of April and May, when the plantations of apple-trees and pear-trees are in blossom. The splendid colouring of this bloom, added to the other tints of nature, form a scene most pleasingly

singly interesting. No view, perhaps, can exceed it for variety and beauty, or more forcibly strike the delighted fancy.

There are several pleasant rides about the Malvern Hills, particularly the Worcester road, from the western ascent of the Hill, to the village of Great Malvern. Here a constant succession of new objects meet the eye of the traveller; something that still awakens his curiosity and attracts notice. He is pleased with the distant prospects, but impressed with mixed ideas of delight and wonder, on viewing that singular variety in the features of nature, which more immediately surrounds him. The luxuriant appearance of the adjoining country, and the barren aspect of the Hills, equally and at once conspicuous, form a striking contrast. The one presents nature in her richest dress,

the

the other nature, romantic, wild, and naked. Each, however, has its peculiar powers to attract the philofophic mind. The former will add delight, and the latter will excite fpeculation.

At the diftance of two miles to the northward is another public road over the Hill, through the Wytch, or Chafm, cut by art in the fummit, in order to fhorten the afcent, and render the paffage over more fafe and eafy. This road is rather fteep and uneven, and therefore feldom ufed for carriages: It is, however, convenient as a fhorter way for travellers on horfeback, from Ledbury to Malvern and Worcefter.

There was a road made about eight years back, by means of which carriages may be taken round the

north

north parts of the Hill. This undertaking was promoted by the late Sir Hildebrand Jacob, Bart. who it is said contributed largely towards defraying the expence of the execution.

The air that we breathe in these rides, and indeed on every part of the Malvern Hills, is very refreshing, has a tendency to create an appetite, and revive the spirits. This pure atmosphere, so stimulating on the Hills, perhaps extends its influence to the surrounding country, where the inhabitants are seldom visited with epidemical diseases.

CHAP.

CHAP IV.

THE SITUATION AND BEAUTY OF GREAT MALVERN DESCRIBED—FOUNDATION OF THE MONASTERY—ACCOUNT OF THE PRESENT CHURCH—ANCIENT VERSES IN PRAISE OF THIS PLACE—SOME ACCOUNT OF LITTLE MALVERN.

THE Village of Great Malvern is moſt delightfully ſituated on the Eaſtern declivity of the Hill, diſtant eight miles from Worceſter, and twenty-two from Cheltenham. It confiſts of about forty houſes, chiefly neat buildings, to which are attached gardens, plantations of fruit-trees, or ſhrubs and evergreens; which render their appearance rural and pretty. Here the aſpect of the

the Hill is peculiarly ſtriking; its bold aſcent, and huge rocks that riſe through the ſurface, have certainly a grand effect, eſpecially in contraſt with the adjoining country, where cultivation and the ſoft beauties of improvement, form the predominant feature.

Here is an Hotel, kept by Mr. Roberts, which ſeems well calculated for the reception of genteel company. It is a neat building, ſituated in the centre of the village, and commands variegated and extenſive proſpects.

Invalids who viſit Malvern, and require greater retirement, may be ſupplied with lodgings, agreeable to their circumſtances, in private families, there being ſeveral who during the ſummer appropriate apartments for the accommodation of ſtrangers.

I have

I have not been able to obtain any manuscripts, which I conceive to be authentic, relative to the antiquities of Malvern; therefore have extracted the following account of the foundation of the Monastery, and its Endowment, from Dr. Nash's History of Worcestershire:

"Before the conquest it was a wilderness thick set with trees, in the midst of which some monks, who aspired to greater perfection, retired from the Priory of Worcester, and became hermits. The enthusiasm spread so fast, that their number soon increased to three hundred, when forming themselves into a Society, they agreed to live according to the order of St. Benedict, and elected Alwin, one of their company, to be superior.— Thus was this Monastery founded about

"about the year 1083, with the con-
"sent and approbation of St. Wolstan,
"Bishop of Worcester. It was de-
"dicated to the Virgin Mary.

"The greatest benefactor was
"Henry I. who gave them Quat
"and Fuleford, in Staffordshire, Hath-
"field, in Herefordshire, and other
"lands. Gislebert, Abbot of West-
"minster, with consent of his Con-
"vent, assigned to them several manors
"and estates; whereupon this Mo-
"nastery was looked upon as a cell,
"or at least subordinate to Westmin-
"ster Abbey.

"Gilbert de Clare Earl of Glou-
"cester, Lord of the Forest, contri-
"buted largely to the revenues of
"this house. Osborn and Richard
"Fitzpontz, or De Pontibus, were
"likewise considerable benefactors.
"Wolstan,

" Wolftan, Prior of Worcefter, with
" confent of his Convent, gave to the
" church of Great Malvern, fundry
" lands in Powick, Braunceford, and
" Leigh.

" Avicot, in Warwickfhire, was a
" cell to Malvern, where were four
" monks. Brockbury likewife, in the
" parifh of Colwall, in Herefordfhire,
" was a cell and contained two
" monks. At the time of the dif-
" folution of the Religious Houfes in
" the reign of Henry VIII. their
" revenue amounted to 318l. 1s. 5½d.
" according to Dugdale; but accord-
" ing to Speed, it was 375l. 0s. 6d. ob.
" It confifted chiefly in the follow-
" ing articles —The manors of New-
" land, Wortefeld, and Powyck, in
" the county of Worcefter; North-
" wode, in Shropfhire; the town of
" Hatfield, and lands in Baldenhale,
                                    " Malvern,

" Malvern, Braunsford, and Lye;
" tythes at Archesfonte, in the diocefe
" of Salifbury, of the yearly value of
" 40s. The Priory of Malvern had
" likewife the appropriate churches of
" Longeney, Powyke, and Malvern;
" the patronage of the churches of
" Hanleye, in the deanery of Powyke,
" of Upton Snodfbury, in the deanery
" of Fayrford in the county of Glo-
" cefter.

" This Priory was granted, 36th
" Henry VIII. to William Pinnocke,
" who alienated it to John Knotes-
" ford, ferjeant-at-arms, whofe daughter
" Ann married William Savage, of
" the family of Savage, of Rock
" Savage, in the county of Chefter;
" from whom, by inheritance, it came
" to Thomas Savage, Efq. of Elmley-
" caftle, in Worcefterfhire. His de-
" fcendant (by a female) Thomas
" Byrche

"Byrche Savage, Esq. sold the demesne to James Oliver, of the city of Worcester, about the year 1774, the scite of the old priory being sold a few years before."

The present Church of Great Malvern was purchased by the inhabitants of John Knotesford, for the sum, it is said, of 200 pounds. It is a magnificent structure, in length one hundred and seventy-one feet, and in breadth sixty-three feet; and the architecture rather light for the age in which it was erected. The tower, which stands near the centre, contains a ring of six bells, and a set of chimes; it is one hundred and twenty-four feet high, and ornamented with pinnacles and battlements of curious workmanship, This church was formerly celebrated for its beautiful windows of stained glass, consisting

ing of various reprefentations, particularly fcripture hiftory; but which is now partly demolifhed. A view, however, of this edifice in its prefent ftate, will convince the obferver of the improved tafte of the architect, and the opulence of its original poffeffors.

Several parts of the choir in this church, are ornamented with a teffellated pavement, containing the coats of arms of many ancient and noble families. Some of thefe panes are in excellent prefervation.

There are numerous monumental infcriptions; but the following are moft worthy of notice.

On the north fide of the communion table is a flat ftone, with this infcription upon it in capitals:

" Here

"Here lyethe the bodye of Penelope, the wife of Robert Walweyn, of Neulande, gentleman, the daughter of Richard Ligon, of Madersfyelde, esquire, the sonne of William Ligon, esquire, sonne of Sir Richard Ligon, knight, the sonne of Thomas Ligon, esquire, and Anne his wife, one of the daughters of the lorde Beauchampe, her mother was Marye, the daughter of Sir Thomas Russell, of Strensham, knyghte. Obiit 13 Januarii, 1596."

On the south side of the choir is an alabaster tomb, on different parts of which are seven figures, said to represent John Knotesford, his wife, and five daughters; and on a pillar adjoining is this inscription:

"Here lieth the body of John Knotesford, esquire, servant to king Henry the VIII. and Jane his wife, daughter to Sir Richard

Richard Knightley, knight, who being firſt marryed to Mr. William Lumley, had iſſue John lord Lumley; and by John Knotesford had iſſue five daughters, and co-heirs; he dyed in the year 1589,—Novem. 23."

Upon a flat ſtone is the following inſcription:

" Siſte, hoſpes pauliſper
Moræ pretium erit te ſire
quæ fœmina ſit hic ſepulta,
Subtus depoſitæ jacent exuviæ Katharinæ
Richardi Daſton de Wormington,
in agro Gloceſtrienſi genere armigeri.
Fucultatis gradu juridici purpurati,
Filiæ familia ſua dignæ;
Ægidii Savage de Elmley Caſtle
in agro Vigornienſi
Armigeri, ex equeſtri ordine oriundi,
Conjugis æque amantis ac redamantæ;

Quæ

Quæ viro suo superstes,
Quo melius Christo soli sponso cælesti nuberet;
Viduam annos quadraginta se continuit:
Eadem in rebus domesticis provida,
Seu Salomonis mater familias illa,
Eleemosynariis larga quasi Dorcas altera,
Divinis pia velut Anna ipsa.
n amicos, familiares, vicinos, advenus omnes,
Amænitate morum suavi prædita,
Mortalitatem exuit, immortalitatem induit
Die anni longissimo in æternitatem translata)
Mensis Junii 11°,
Anno Christi 1674, ætatis suæ 84.
Effigiem habet Elmley supramemorata
(Una cum conjugis prolisque sculptilibus)
Cœlum animam, sepulerum corpus,
Exemplum superstites ac posteri;
Δι αυτῆς αποθανὼν ετι λαλεῖται
Dat mundus famam virtuti, dat pietati
Aureolam, cœlum, vivit utroque loco."

F   " Margaret,

In different parts of the choir are these inscriptions:

" Margaret, late wife of William Lygon, Esq. and only child of Thomas Corbyn, Esq. obiit 21 Oct. 1699, ætat. 42."

" William Lygon, junior, of Madresfield, Esquire, obiit 4 September 1716, ætatis 26."

" Here lies the body of William Ligon, of Madresfield, Esq. who departed this life 16 day of March, anno Dom. 1720, ætatis suæ 79."

" Hic jacet Maria, uxor Gulielmi Ligon de Madresfield, armigeri, filia Francisci Egiocke, de Egiocke, militis, et cohæres fratris.—Obiit decimo Novembris 1668, ætatis suæ 59."

At the bottom of the stone are these lines:

"Stay,

" Stay, paffenger, and from this dufty urne
Both what I was, and what thou muft be, learne:
Grace, virtue, beauty had no priviledge,
That everlafting ftatute to abridge,
That all muft dye; then, gentle friend, with care
In life for death and happinefs prepare.
 Flebilis hoc pofuit thalami confors,
 Mortuus eft Januarii 29, 1680,
 Ætatis fexagefimo octavo."

" To the dear memory of Richard Lygon, of Madresfield, in the county of Worcefter, who departed this mortal life, April 15, 1687, in the 49th year of his age: Anne, his forrowful wife, eldeft daughter to Sir Francis Ruffell, of the fame county, Bart. dedicates this."—

" Here refteth the body of Elizabeth, the wife of John Wallfam, Efqr. and daughter to William Lygon, Efqr. who departed this transitory life the 12th day of April, anno Dom. 1674."

"John Woodehouse, Esqr. third son of Sir Philip Woodehouse, of Kimberly, in Norfolk, Baronet, died 26 June, 1718, aged 62 years."

"John Dickins, of Bobinton, in the county of Stafford, Esq. buried April 25, 1656, aged 78 years and 6 months."

"Richard Brindley, died 30 January, 1714, aged 29 years; also Richard, son of the above-named Richard and Anne his wife, died Feb. 9, 1719, aged 6 years and 9 months."

Towards the west end of the church is a flat stone, with the following inscription upon it in capitals. It was dug up in a garden adjoining to to the church, in the year 1711, and is the epitaph of Walcher, who was the second Prior of Malvern.

" Philosophus dignus bonus astrologos lotheringus, vir pius ac humilis, monachus prior hujus ovilis, hic jacet in cista geometricus ac abacista, Doctor Walcherus; flet plebs dolet undqive clerus; huic lux prima mori dedit octobris seniori; vivat ut in cœlis exhoret quifque fidelis. 1135.',

The following eulogium of Great Malvern, and its waters, is said to have been composed by the Parish Clerk about the year 1590, from which time it remained in manuscript till 1778, when it was published in the History of Worcestershire. It is, however, I believe, not very generally known, and therefore may prove acceptable to many of my readers.

As I did walk alone
   Late in an evening;
I heard the voice of one
   Moſt ſweetly ſinging;
Which did delight me much,
Becauſe the ſong was ſuch,
And ended with a touch,
         O praiſe the Lord.

The God of ſea and land
   That rules above us,
Stays his avenging hand;
   Cauſe he doth love us;
And doth his bleſſings ſend,
Altho' we do offend:
Then let us all amend,
         And praiſe the Lord.

Great Malvern on a rock,
   Thou ſtandeſt ſurely,

Do not thyself forget,
  Living securely:
Thou haft of bleffings ftore,
No country town hath more,
Do not forget therefore,
           To praife the Lord.

Thou haft a famous church
  And rarely builded:
No country town hath fuch
  Moft men have yielded.
For pillars ftout and ftrong,
And windows large and long:
Remember in thy fong,
           To praife the Lord.

There is God's fervice read
  With rev'rence duely:
There is his word preached,
  Learned and truely:
And every fabbath day
Singing of Pfalms they fay,
Its furely the only way
           To praife the Lord.

The fun in glory great,
   When firft it rifeth,
Doth blefs thy happy feat,
   And thee advifeth,
That then its time to pray,
That God may blefs thy way,
And keep thee all the day,
            To praife the Lord.

That thy profpect is good,
   None can deny thee;
Thou haft great ftore of wood
   Growing hard by thee:
Which is a bleffing great
To roaft and boil thy meat,
And thee in cold to heat,
            O praife the Lord.

Preferve it I advife
   Whilft thou haft it;
Spare not in any wife,
   But do not wafte it:
                        Leaft

Left thou repent too late,
Remember Hanley's fate,
In time ſhut up thy gate,
    And praiſe the Lord.

A chaſe for royal deer
 Round doth beſet thee;
Too many I do fear
 For aught they get thee,
Yet tho' they eat away
Thy corn, thy graſs, and hay,
Doe not forget, I ſay,
    To praiſe the Lord.

That noble chaſe doth give
 Thy beaſts their feeding;
Where they in ſummer live,
 With little heeding:
Thy ſheep and Swine there go,
So doth thy horſe alſo,
Till winter brings in ſnow:
    Then praiſe the Lord.

      Turn

Turn up thine eyes on high,
 There fairly ſtanding,
See Malvern's higheſt hill,
 All hills commanding;
They all confeſs at will,
Their ſovereign Malvern Hill,
Let it be mighty ſtill!
      O praiſe the Lord.

When weſtern winds doth rock
 Both town and country,
Thy hill doth break the ſhock,
 They cannot hurt thee;
When waters great abound
And many a country's drown'd
Thou ſtandeſt ſafe and ſound,
      O praiſe the Lord.

Out of that famous hill
 There daily ſpringeth
A water, paſſing ſtill
 Which always bringeth
      Great

Great comfort to all them
That are diseased men,
And makes them well again,
>To praise the Lord.

Hast thou a wound to heal,
  The which doth grieve thee?
Come then unto this well,
  It will relieve thee;
Noli me tangeres,
And other maladies,
Have here their remedies,
>Prais'd be the Lord.

To drink thy waters, store
  Lie in thy bushes,
Many with ulcers sore,
  Many with bruises;
Who succour find from ill,
By money given still,
Thanks to the Christian will:
>O praise the Lord.

>A thou-

A thoufand bottles there,
　　Were filled weekly,
And many coftrils rare
　　For ftomachs ficly;
Some of them into Kent,
Some were to London fent,
Others to Berwick went,
　　　　　　O praife the Lord.

LITTLE

LITTLE MALVERN, is situated in the county of Worcester, distant about three miles and a half from Great Malvern, and one and a half from the Holy Well. It lies on a *recumbent* slope, near the entrance of a great recess in the Hill, and was formerly a considerable village, though now it consists of only a few houses. No longer back than the reign of Queen Elizabeth, the parish contained 37 families, which number is now diminished to six.

Here was likewise a Monastery, but not so magnificent as the above mentioned.—Dr. Nash says:

"It was founded for the same
" cause, and in the same manner, as
" the

" the neighbouring Priory. A con-
" gregation of monks, of the Priory
" of Worcester, having entered into
" the wilderneſs of Malvern, and de-
" termined to lead an auſtere life as
" hermits.—Jocelin and Edred, of the
" order of St. Benedict, are ſaid to
" have founded, and dedicated this
" houſe and church to St. Gyles,
" about the year 1171.

" The principal benefactors were
" William de Blois, and King Henry
" II. Gilbert de Clare, Earl of
" Glouceſter, Lord of Malvern Chace,
" was alſo a conſiderable contri-
" butor.

" At the diſſolution the revenues
" of this houſe, according to Dugdale,
" were eſtimated at 98l. 10s. 9d.—
" But according to Speed, they
" amounted to 102l. 10s. 9d.
" The

" The diffolved Monaftery, with
" the lands, perpetual advowfon of
" the church of Little Malvern, &c.
" were granted by Philip and Mary
" to John Ruffell."*

Little Malvern Church, which is now partly in ruins, was rebuilt about the year 1482, by John Alcock, Bifhop of Worcefter.—It was ornamented with windows of ftained glafs, little of which is now left.— The floor exhibits the remains of a teffellated pavement; and on a beam is a piece of carving of moft exquifite workmanfhip; but there are few monumental infcriptions.

---

* This was a branch of the Ruffell's of Strenfham, the heirefs of which was married to Thomas Williams, Efq. of Trellynnie, in the county of Flint, in whofe family it now continues.

Near the church is an antique building, the property and refidence of Mifs Williams, fituated on the fpot where ftood the ancient Monaftery. This houfe, which has lately undergone confiderable improvements, has in front a fine piece of water, and commands various and beautiful profpects. The declivity of the adjoining glen, clothed with bold impending wood, and the hill receding above, afford an appearance from hence pleafingly romantic. To the eaftward lies an expanfe of fertile meadows, variegated with trees, which add much to the beauty of this fituation. This fequeftered fpot, viewed as a whole, either from the hill above or the plain beneath, equally attracts attention. Here art has a venerable afpect given it by time; and nature is rendered pleafing by its exuberance and charming fimplicity.

CHAP.

CHAP V.

A SKETCH OF THE COUNTRY, AND CONCISE ACCOUNT OF THE GENTLEMEN's SEATS, SCENERY, AND PICTURESQUE VIEWS, IN THE ENVIRONS OF THE MALVERN HILLS.

THE country lying on the weſt-ſide of the Malvern Hills, is remarkable for the large plantation of apple-trees and pear-trees, and their conſequent productions of cyder and perry; particularly the former, which in general is rich and fine taſted. However, it may be proper to obſerve, that there is in moſt places a manifeſt ſuperiority in the quality of the fruit, and conſequently of the liquor, produced on the low ground, over that which grows on the elevated.—This difference originates from the nature of the foil, which, on the low ground, is a ftrong clay; on the banks a light earth mixed with gravel, which in fome places is incumbent on limeftone. It is well known that the fruit produced on the former foil, affords the liquor in general rich and pleafant; but on the latter more pale and acid.

On the eaft fide of the Hills in the county of Worcefter, lies a large tract of Common, which together with other land adjoining, conftituted the ancient *Malvern Chace*: the greateft part of which, in the time of William the Conqueror, abounded with large grown wood. This Foreft, or Chace, which was plentifully ftocked with deer, belonged to the Crown in the reign of King Edward I. who gave it to
Gilbert

Gilbert de Clare, Earl of Gloucester. Before the Earl had been long in poffeffion, he had a difpute with the Bifhop of Hereford, relating to the weftern boundary; to end which, and render the divifion permanent, he caufed a great ditch to be made along the ridge of the Hills, many parts of which are now in good prefervation. After the death of the Earl the poffeffion of the Chace was retained by his fucceffors for feveral ages, and then became again the property of the Crown. In the year 1690, a grant was made of one-third of it to Richard Heath, and Sir Cornelius Vermyden, Knight; and the other two-thirds to the adjoining Parifhes. It was afterwards declared free from the foreft laws by an act of parliament made the fixteenth of King Charles II. Since that period there have been feveral trials refpecting the right of common, all which were

termi-

terminated, so as ultimately to establish that privilege (with very few exceptions) equally among the inhabitants of thirteen parishes, which are situated upon the confines of the ancient Chace. That part of the Common, which is in the parish of Hanley Castle, it is expected will shortly be inclosed,* agreeable to an act of parliament, lately obtained for that purpose.

The beauty, fertility, and inviting appearance of the country around the Malvern

* Should that take place the admirer of natural beauty will have to regret the loss of its present picturesque effect.—But an accession of cultivated land, and consequently, a greater production of wheat, will undoubtedly be deemed an ample compensation; especially at the present time, when the scarcity of that article, is so severely felt by the lower classes of society.

Malvern Hills, have induced people of diſtinction and property to make it their reſidence: Hence the face of nature is diverſified with ſome very capital houſes; and its ſimplicity embelliſhed with elegant improvement. Some of theſe reſidences, together with their reſpective ſituations, deſerve particular notice.

In a retired valley, on the weſt-ſide of the pariſh of Colwall, in the county of Hereford, diſtant about three miles from the Malvern Wells, is *Hope-End*, the ſeat of Sir Henry Tempeſt, Bart. This is partly a modern ſtructure, rather large and commodious, ſome of the apartments are highly finiſhed. It is nearly ſurrounded by ſmall eminences, and therefore does not command any diſtant proſpect, except to the ſouthward, nor is that very extenſive; but this defect is compenſated by the various and beautiful ſcenery

scenery that immediately surrounds this secluded residence. In front of the house are some fine pieces of water; on their banks are planted a variety of shrubs and evergreens, which, in conjunction with the water, look very ornamental. The deer park, which is a small but pleasant tract, lies on the ascent of the contiguous eminences, whose projecting parts, and bending declivities, modelled by nature, display much beauty. It contains an elegant profusion of wood, disposed in the most careless yet pleasing order. Much of the park, and its scenery, is in view from the house, where it presents a very agreeable appearance.

In the above deer park is an ash of remarkable growth, which is now in an improving state. It is the largest I have ever seen, and, perhaps, the largest in Britain.

In the parish of Colwall is also a pretty residence, the property of Richard Brydges, Esq. This house is pleasantly situated at the eastern foot of an eminence, which abounds with wood, interspersed with cultivated fields and pastures. On various parts of this eminence grows a considerable quantity of fir, whose gloomy aspect displays a kind of solemn grandeur. The gardens, which are contiguous to the house, are well situated. Springs of water rise at a small distance, affording a plentiful supply for use or ornament. However, not all the attention has been paid to the latter, which a situation thus circumstanced seems to merit. From hence is a pleasing view of the neighbourhood, terminated by the Malvern Hills, which are about two miles distant.

About

About one mile diſtant from the Malvern Wells, is a neat villa, called *Brand-Green Lodge*, late the reſidence of Colonel Roberts. It ſtands on the weſtern declivity of a pleaſant part of the Malvern Hills, on a ſituation elevated about five hundred feet from the level. From this romantic ſpot, is a fine view of the camp, which is about half a mile diſtant, and a very extenſive proſpect to the weſtward. It is not affected with that greater degree of cold peculiar to elevated ſituations, being happily ſheltered from the eaſt and north winds; from the former by the Malvern Hills, and from the latter by woods that lie at an agreeable diſtance. The front of the houſe is white, and ſhaded by a range of evergreens, which gives it a picturefque appearance.

At Eastnor, in the county of Hereford, distant four miles from the Malvern Wells, is *Castleditch*, the seat of Lord Somers. The greatest part of this house is an ancient building, to which have lately been added, several elegant apartments built of free-stone, on a modern plan. Its situation, being a flat, loses the advantage of a distant prospect; but the projecting declivities of the Malvern Hills, and other eminences, with which it is environed, being ornamented with a profusion of wood, display a pleasing scene of rural beauty. The park, which surrounds the house, is not very extensive, but well stocked with deer, prettily diversified with trees, and adorned with a fine piece of water. —In one part is a small elevation, whereon is erected a summer-house, that commands an extensive prospect to the southward. The gardens are well

well situated, laid out with taste, and kept in excellent order. From several positions, at a small distance to the eastward, the house and contiguous scenery have a pleasing effect; the latter being devoid of that formal regularity in the disposition of its parts which often disfigures the scene it is intended to embellish.

A beautiful road extends from the Malvern Hills to Castleditch, along the summit of a small elevation called the Ridgeway, from different parts of which much beauty is visible in several directions. Here the grand elevation of the Hill, its descent clothed with wood, and the valley beneath interspersed with fertile pastures, arrest the attention, and delight the fancy of the beholder. In several parts of this natural terrace are a variety of evergreens, the spontaneous produce of its decli-

declivity, whereon the eye repofes with much pleafure, after pervading diftant objects, and more romantic fcenery.

Near the fouthern extremity of the Malvern Hills is *Bromfberow-Place*, formerly the refidence of Colonel Walter Yate, and now the property of W. H. Yate, Efq. This is a handfome fpacious building, containing many excellent apartments, fome of them finifhed in a ftile of tafte and elegance. A gravel walk through a fhrubbery, on the confines of a beautiful lawn, leads to the gardens, the walls of which are concealed from the manfion by the form of the intervening ground, fo as not to intercept the profpect, nor break the line of beauty. The houfe itfelf makes a good appearance, but the foreground, which is divided from the lawn by a funk fence, feems to call for a border of shrubs, or ornamental wood, in order to render it more picturesque. The prospects from hence are variegated and beautiful, and to the southward very extensive, being terminated by distant hills in Glocestershire. Some small protuberances, enriched with plantations, seen over a varied ground, adorn the western prospect. Here are also seen the Malvern Hills facing an eminence clothed with hanging wood, the view of which is very pleasing.

In the parish of Handley-Castle, and county of Worcester, distant about two miles from the Malvern Wells, is *Blackmore Park*, the seat of Thomas Hornyold, Esq. This is a modern and elegant finished structure, the situation dry and pleasant, but its prospects are not very extensive. In the adjacent grounds is a large quantity of of fine elm, planted uniformly in rows; but a plantation thus difpofed, though exceeding pretty in itfelf, does not afford that picturefque appearance to a diftant beholder, as groups of trees detached at various diftances. In the neighbourhood are feveral large pieces of water, the property of the above gentleman, which are not unworthy of notice.

In the parifh of Maddersfield, and county of Worcefter, diftant about four miles from the Malvern Wells, is an antique but neat building, the refidence of William Lygon, Efq.— Its fituation is rather flat, but commands fome good views, particularly of a fmall eminence, lying about a mile to the eaftward, containing fine plantations, which produce a beautiful effect. There is, likewife, a view of the Malvern Hills, the village of Great

Malvern

Malvern and parts adjacent. The grounds contiguous to the manſion are enriched with fine wood, and rendered various and pretty by well-formed pieces of water. Very near to the houſe is Maddersfield Chapel, encircled by a range of trees, which together affords an appearance quite piƈtureſque.

CONTENTS.

CHAP. I.

The Situation, Extent and Height of the Malvern Hills described—Some Account of their component Matter—Conjecture respecting their State in remote Antiquity—Sketch of their Surface.

CHAP. II.

An Account of the Camps—Dimensions of a Cave in the Hill—Particulars of the Discovery of a Coronet, or Crown of Gold—Description of Bransil Castle.

CHAP III.

Of the Holy Well, the Efficacy of its Water, and the Method of using it—Some other Springs taken notice of—Description of the Lodging-house—Extent and Beauty of the Prospects from the

the Malvern Hills—Account of the Rides in their Vicinity.

CHAP. IV.

The Situation and Beauty of Great Malvern defcribed—Foundation of the Monaftery—Account of the prefent Church—Antient Verfes in praife of the Place—Some Account of Little Malvern.

CHAP. V.

A Sketch of the Country, and concife Account of the Gentlemen's Seats, Scenery, and Picturefque Views, in the Environs of the Malvern Hills.

www.ingramcontent.com/pod-product-compliance
Lightning Source LLC
Chambersburg PA
CBHW020323090426
42735CB00009B/1374